A Walk
in the
Boreal
Forest

by Rebecca L. Johnson

with illustrations by Phyllis V. Saroff

CAROLRHODA BOOKS, INC./MINNEAPOLIS

For my niece Claire, who helps me see
the world with fresh eyes
                                    —*R. L. J.*

Carolrhoda Books, Inc.
A division of Lerner Publishing Group
241 First Avenue North
Minneapolis, Minnesota 55401 U.S.A.

Website address: www.lernerbooks.com

Library of Congress Cataloging-in-Publication Data

Johnson, Rebecca L.
  A walk in the boreal forest / by Rebecca L. Johnson; illustrations
by Phyllis V. Saroff
    p.   cm. — (Biomes of North America)
  Includes index.
  Summary: Describes the climate, seasons, plants, animals, and soil
of the boreal forest, a biome or land zone, which stretches across the
northern parts of North America, Europe, and Asia.
  ISBN 1-57505-156-7 (lib. bdg. : alk. paper)
1. Taiga ecology—Juvenile literature. 2. Taigas—Juvenile literature.
[1. Taigas. 2. Forest ecology. 3. Ecology.] I. Saroff, Phyllis V., ill. II.
Title. III Series: Johnson, Rebecca L. Biomes of North America
QH541.5.T3 J65 2001
577.3'7—dc21   00-008240

Manufactured in the United States of America
1 2 3 4 5 6 – JR – 06 05 04 03 02 01

Words
to Know

ALGAE (Al-jee)—plant-like living things

BACTERIA (bak-TEE-ree-uh)—microscopic, one-celled living things found almost everywhere

BIOME (BYE-ohm)—a major community of living things that covers a large area, such as a grassland or a forest

BOG (bawg)—a patch of spongy, soggy ground

BOREAL (BOHR-ee-uhl)—northern

CLIMATE (KLYE-mut)— a region's usual pattern of weather over a long period of time

CONE SCALES—small, overlapping parts of a cone such as a pinecone

CONIFERS (KAH-nih-furz)—plants that produce seeds inside cones

DECIDUOUS (duh-SIH-juh-wuhs)—falling off. Deciduous plants lose their leaves at the end of the growing season.

FUNGI (FUHN-gye)—living things, such as mushrooms and molds, that get their food by breaking down dead plant and animal matter

HIBERNATE (HYE-bur-nate)—to pass the winter in a special deep sleep

LICHENS (LYE-kenz)—small, crusty living things made up of fungi and algae growing together

MARSH—an area of wet, low-lying land near a pond or lake

PREDATORS (PREH-duh-turz)—animals that hunt and eat other animals

PREY (pray)—animals that are hunted and eaten by other animals

RESIN (REH-zihn)—sticky tree sap

filtering through the pines

A deer wanders quietly among stately pine trees. He bends down to nibble a fern. Suddenly, a pinecone falls from the treetops. It lands with a thump on the ground. Startled, the deer leaps back. With a snort, he disappears into the dark green shadows of the boreal forest.

Like a dark green carpet, millions of spruce trees cover gently rolling hills in the boreal forest.

The boreal forest is a wild place in the far north. Boreal means "northern." Millions and millions of trees grow close together in this huge forest. Like wooden soldiers, they stand side by side, straight and tall.

The boreal forest stretches across the northern parts of North America, Europe, and Asia. It forms a nearly unbroken belt of trees that circles the Earth.

Most of the trees in this forest are conifers, such as spruce, pine, and fir. Conifers are trees that make cones.

Most conifers have needle-shaped leaves. They keep their needles year-round. Because of this, most conifers are always green. So they are also called "evergreens."

Evergreens are quite different from deciduous trees, such as oak, maple, and elm. The leaves of deciduous trees fall off every autumn. New leaves grow every spring.

Needle-shaped conifer leaves come in many shapes and sizes.

hemlock

larch

spruce

pine

Cones on a spruce tree are clustered near the tip of a branch.

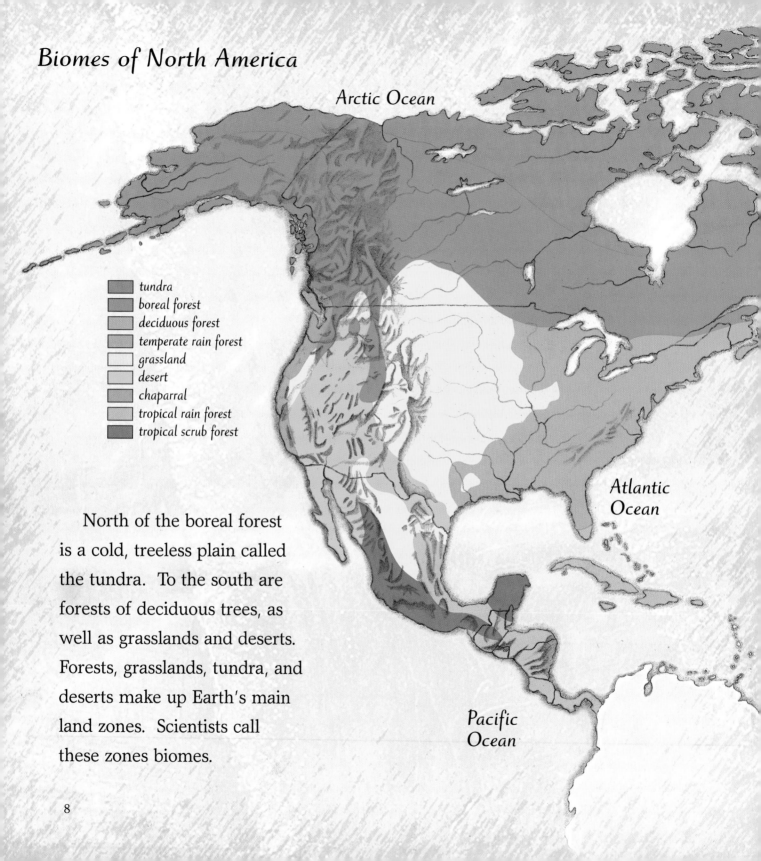

Biomes of North America

Arctic Ocean

▨	tundra
▨	boreal forest
▨	deciduous forest
▨	temperate rain forest
▨	grassland
▨	desert
▨	chaparral
▨	tropical rain forest
▨	tropical scrub forest

Atlantic Ocean

Pacific Ocean

North of the boreal forest is a cold, treeless plain called the tundra. To the south are forests of deciduous trees, as well as grasslands and deserts. Forests, grasslands, tundra, and deserts make up Earth's main land zones. Scientists call these zones biomes.

Each biome has a different type of climate. The climate is an area's usual pattern of weather over a long period of time.

Every biome is home to a special group of plants. The plants are well suited to living in that climate and to growing in the soil found there.

Only a few kinds of trees grow in the boreal forest. But there are many of each kind.

Like many animals in the boreal forest, crossbills (left) depend on conifers for much of their food.

Snow covers the boreal forest in winter (right).

Every biome is also home to a special group of animals. In one way or another, the animals depend on the plants to survive. Many of a biome's animals eat plants. Other animals eat the plant-eaters.

All the plants and animals in a biome form a community. In that community, every living thing depends on other community members to survive. A biome's climate, soil, plants, and animals are all connected this way.

The boreal forest has a fairly cold climate. During the long winter, heavy snow blankets the forest. The temperature often drops below zero. Winter days are very short. At midwinter, the sun shines only about six hours each day.

Cool green light fills the forest as sunshine filters down through the fir trees.

Summer in the boreal forest is cool and pleasant. Summer lasts only three to four months, but the days are long and bright. The sun shines from very early in the morning until late at night.

Summer rains make the boreal forest a damp place. Among the tall trees are many ponds and marshes and bogs. A bog is a patch of ground that is always wet and spongy.

Grasses and wild-flowers surround a small bog in an open space among the trees.

Trunks of red pines crowd in from every direction. Here and there, sunbeams push back the shadows.

A late summer rain shower has just ended. Raindrops still drip from the trees. Let's take a walk and discover what life in the boreal forest is like.

The clean, sharp scent of evergreens fills the air. It smells like freshly cut Christmas trees. Tall, straight trunks surround you. There are only a few kinds of trees, mostly spruce, fir, pine, hemlock, and larch.

High above your head, the treetops are so close together that they block out most of the sunlight. Down on the shadowy forest floor, the crowded trunks all look very much the same. You could easily get lost in this forest.

White spruce trees are common in the boreal forest. They can grow up to 150 feet tall—almost as tall as four school buses stacked end to end!

As you walk along, squirrels and chipmunks chatter in the trees. Birds call to each other. But you are making hardly any sound at all. The ground is covered with a thick layer of dead conifer needles. This carpet of needles is soft and springy and quiet.

The dim light and the thick layer of needles make it difficult for most plants to grow on the forest floor. There are a few shrubs. Frilly ferns unfurl in the shadows. Clumps of soft moss sprout here and there. Lichens grow on tree branches and trunks.

A red squirrel snacks in the treetops (above). Colorful lichens share living space with feather moss (right). Small shrubs line a needle-covered path through the trees (far right).

Dig down through the thick needle carpet until you reach the soil. It is cool and damp. Worms, fungi, and bacteria live on needles, cones, and branches that have fallen on the forest floor. They break all this dead matter into smaller pieces and turn it into soil. The soil feeds the plants and helps them grow. Conifers grow well in this soil.

Wintergreen (above), with its bright red berries, thrives on the damp forest floor. A spruce seedling grows beside a clump of moss (right).

Conifer needles contain a kind of sap called resin. So does the bark of conifer trees. See the small cut in the trunk of that pine tree? There's resin oozing out. Sniff it. It smells like turpentine. Touch it. It's incredibly sticky.

Resin tastes terrible. So it protects the trees from plant-eaters in the forest. Most animals won't even nibble on conifer needles or bark.

The spruce grouse is one of the few animals, besides insects, that eats conifer needles.

Sticky resin oozes from a wound in the bark of a conifer.

If you sliced a pinecone in half, you'd see how the seeds lie between the scales of the cone.

But many forest animals feast on conifer seeds. The seeds don't contain resin. Conifer seeds are hidden inside the cones hanging from the branches overhead. More cones lie scattered on the forest floor.

Seed-eaters are busy all around you. Hear that rustling sound? A red-backed vole scurries across the ground. He tugs at a fallen cone with tiny paws, pulling out the seeds hidden between the hard cone scales.

A red-backed vole searches for seeds on the forest floor.

Many conifer seeds have papery "wings." When the wind blows, the seeds can travel far.

Two deer mice come bounding out from behind a fern. Their pointed noses twitch as they sniff out conifer seeds among the fallen needles. Ground squirrels zip back and forth. Their cheeks are stuffed with seeds. A woodchuck lumbers past, looking for a meal.

Deer mice are also called white-footed mice. They eat mostly seeds.

Half-eaten cones and cone scales pile up under branches where squirrels sit and eat. These piles are called squirrel middens.

A red squirrel uses sharp front teeth and claws to tear apart cones (*above right*).

Red squirrels are perched in the treetops above you. They are tearing apart cones with their teeth and paws. Squirrels eat a lot of conifer seeds. But they don't eat all the seeds they find. They hide many seeds under logs and in holes in tree trunks. These stored seeds will be food for the squirrels during the long winter ahead.

Birds like conifer seeds, too. In the branches just above your head, crossbills hop among clusters of cones. Look closely at the beaks of these small birds.

A crossbill uses its strange-looking beak to pry cone scales apart.

See how the tips cross over each other? A crossbill's beak looks very strange. But it's the perfect tool for prying cone scales apart to reach the seeds inside.

Gray jays and Clark's nutcrackers use their large, strong beaks to tear cones apart. Nutcrackers store thousands of seeds in holes in the ground. Both the birds and the trees are helped by this. The birds have food for the winter, and the trees get some of their seeds "planted" in the soil. Some of these seeds grow into new trees.

With its long, sharp beak, a Clark's nutcracker (above left) digs pine seeds from their cones. The bird also has a pouch under its tongue for carrying seeds.

23

A nuthatch searches for caterpillars and beetles hiding under loose tree bark.

A magnolia warbler perches on his nest in a fir tree (above right).

Many of the birds you hear are summer visitors to the boreal forest. In the spring, ruby-crowned kinglets, warblers, and dozens of other kinds of birds fly up from the south. They build nests in the tall conifers. Some birds are seed-eaters. But others eat insects. During the summer, insects thrive in the damp boreal forest. Mosquitoes and blackflies swarm among the trees.

Rat-ta-tat! Rat-ta-tata-tat! Clinging to the trunk of an old spruce tree is a three-toed woodpecker. It hammers its strong beak into the wood. It is searching for beetles that hide beneath the bark.

During the summer, the boreal forest is full of blackflies that bite and suck blood. Blackflies are about as large as the head of a pin.

A three-toed woodpecker arrives at its tree-hole nest. Can you see the baby woodpeckers peeking out?

Perched in the top branches of the same spruce tree, a great gray owl sits like a statue. Only its eyes move as it scans the ground for voles and chipmunks. Other predators patrol the forest, too. Goshawks hunt smaller birds. Sleek pine martens chase squirrels through the treetops. Red foxes lie hidden, ready to pounce on any small animal that passes by.

A great gray owl stares down from the treetops (left). From a lofty perch in a pine tree, a marten watches for prey (above).

A snowshoe hare hops out from behind a spruce tree. It is looking for grass or leaves or twigs to eat. In its summer coat of brown fur, the hare is very hard to see against the forest floor.

Snowshoe hares have gray-brown fur in summer. In winter, their fur turns pure white to match the snow.

In winter, a lynx's furry feet leave soft-edged prints in the snow.

Suddenly, the hare sees you. It thumps away on big hind feet. Snowshoe hares are always on the lookout for danger. They are hunted by foxes, owls, and lynxes. Lynxes are the only members of the cat family that live in the boreal forest. They pad silently among the trees on huge paws.

Muscles tensed, a Canadian lynx is ready to pounce. It may have found a snowshoe hare.

29

Beavers use their large front teeth to gnaw wood and cut down trees. When you see stumps like this one, you know beavers live nearby.

Surrounded by water, a beaver lodge is out of the reach of most predators.

Up ahead, through the spruce trees, is a pond. Aspen, willow, and birch trees line its banks. These are deciduous trees. You can find them here and there in the forest. Their bright green leaves stand out against the darker green of the conifers.

See how some of the aspens have been cut down? Their narrow trunks have been neatly chewed, leaving a pointed stump. A brown, whiskered head bobs up in the water. The beaver swims past you and crawls out onto the bank.

Beavers live in domed lodges. They use mud and sticks to build these lodges in the middle of lakes and ponds. Beavers eat the leaves, twigs, and bark of deciduous trees. All summer long, they cut down aspen and birch trees with their chisel-like teeth. They snip off branches and store them underwater as food for the coming winter.

A beaver tows a freshly cut branch. It will store the branch underwater near its lodge. Beavers are good swimmers, with webbed hind feet and a large, flat tail.

A mother moose checks on her young calf. Moose are the largest members of the deer family.

There are hoofprints on the bank. Deer and elk have been drinking from the pond.

On the far side of the pond, two dark shapes step out of the trees. They are a mother moose and her calf. They munch on aspen leaves and willow twigs.

Suddenly, a black bear appears on the bank. The mother moose snorts loudly. The bear is a threat to her calf. But the bear ignores the moose. He ambles through the raspberry bushes on the bank, gobbling up ripe berries.

Ripe berries make a sweet meal for a cinnamon-colored black bear. Grizzly bears, which are much larger than black bears, also live in parts of the boreal forest.

The mother moose goes back to eating. She would be more nervous if there were wolves nearby. Wolves roam in packs through the forest. They hunt as a team.

A large gray wolf stops for a drink (right).
A moose calf stays close to its mother (below).
A calf on its own is an easy target for predators.

Large feet and long claws help make wolverines good climbers.

Pound for pound, the wolverine is the most ferocious predator in the boreal forest. A wolverine is about the size of a small, but strongly built, dog. It has short, sturdy legs, thick fur, long claws, and big teeth. Wolverines are quite rare. You would be lucky to see one. But if you did, you'd want to keep your distance.

A snarling wolverine shows a mouthful of sharp teeth. Wolverines are strong enough to kill animals much larger than themselves.

This time of year, there is the threat of fire in the boreal forest. Lightning often starts forest fires. The dead needles on the forest floor are full of resin, which catches fire easily.

Many trees are killed in forest fires. But fires give the surviving trees more room to grow. The ashes are rich food for all kinds of plants. And some types of cones must be heated by fire before they will release their seeds. If the cones don't release their seeds, the seeds can't grow.

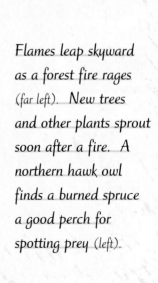

Conifer seedlings grow very slowly. A four-year-old fir tree is only ankle-high.

Flames leap skyward as a forest fire rages (far left). New trees and other plants sprout soon after a fire. A northern hawk owl finds a burned spruce a good perch for spotting prey (left).

Boreal chickadees tuck seeds into moss and lichens growing on tree branches. In winter, the chickadees come back and eat these hidden meals.

These late-summer days are sunny and pleasant. But change is coming. By the end of August, morning frosts nip the air, warning the summer birds that it is time to fly south to warmer places. The leaves of the aspen, willow, and birch turn blazing gold and scatter in the wind.

By September, the summer birds have left. The forest is almost silent. Only owls, woodpeckers, and a few other kinds of birds stay behind to face the long winter.

Golden aspen leaves glow in the autumn sun (left). Spruce grouse live in the boreal forest all year long (above left).

Caribou search for lichens beneath the snow.

As it gets colder and the days become shorter, great herds of caribou arrive. All summer long, the caribou roam across the tundra. But as winter approaches, they migrate south to the boreal forest. Here they are sheltered from the wind by the tall trees and can find enough food to eat.

Birds stay warm in winter by puffing up their feathers. They also perch in sheltered places, out of the wind.

As winter tightens its grip, the beaver pond freezes over. Snow falls day after day. It covers the forest with a thick white blanket that will last until spring.

The animals that live year-round in the boreal forest survive the long, cold winter in different ways. Birds have fluffy feathers to keep them warm. Wolves, foxes, and caribou have thick coats of fur or hair.

Snow and cold don't bother the red fox. Its coat of thick fur keeps it warm during the winter.

41

Beaver lodges are built of sticks and mud. The beavers leave the lodge through tunnels that lead into the water.

Red squirrels survive the long winter by eating the food they stored during the summer months.

Some animals hunt. Others live on stored food. Squirrels and nutcrackers eat the seeds they hoarded all summer. Out in the ice-covered pond, the beavers are safe inside their lodge. When they are hungry, they bring branches up from the bottom of the pond to eat.

Mice and voles scamper through tunnels they dig in the deep snow. They eat seeds and stems they find on the forest floor.

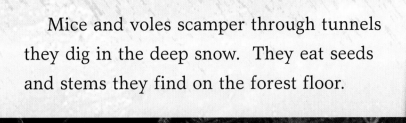

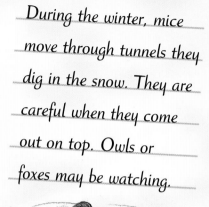

During the winter, mice move through tunnels they dig in the snow. They are careful when they come out on top. Owls or foxes may be watching.

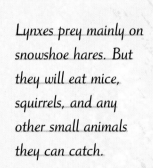

Lynxes prey mainly on snowshoe hares. But they will eat mice, squirrels, and any other small animals they can catch.

Safe from winter's bitter cold, a hibernating woodchuck lies curled up inside its underground, grass-lined burrow.

Snow slides off the down-slanting branches of conifers.

Black bears, fat from many autumn meals, sleep in snug dens. But they wake up quickly if they're disturbed.

A few animals do more than just sleep. They hibernate. Curled up in underground burrows, woodchucks and ground squirrels fall into a special deep "sleep." Their hearts beat very slowly. They breathe very slowly, too. They hibernate until spring, when it begins to get warm.

Far above the hibernators, wind sighs through the tops of the tall conifers. Like the animals, the trees can withstand winter. Their needles have a waxy coating that keeps them from drying out in the cold wind. Their branches slant downward, so heavy snow slides right off.

Winter is long and harsh, but the great trees stand tall. And in the spring, they will again make the cones and seeds on which so much life in the boreal forest depends.

At home among the trees, a large male white-tailed deer heads deeper into the boreal forest.

for further
Information
about the Boreal Forest

Books

DuTemple, Lesley A. *Moose.* Minneapolis: Lerner, 1998.

——. *North American Moose.* Minneapolis: Carolrhoda, 2001.

Fraggalosch, Audrey. *Northern Refuge: A Story of a Canadian Boreal Forest.* Norwalk, CT: Soundprints, 1999.

Green, Jen. *A Dead Log.* New York: Crabtree, 1999.

Holmes, Bonnie. *Quaking Aspen.* Minneapolis: Carolrhoda, 1999.

Johnson, Sylvia A. *Songbirds: The Language of Song.* Minneapolis: Carolrhoda, 2001.

Lepthien, Emilie U. *Beavers.* Chicago: Children's Press, 1992.

——. *Squirrels.* Chicago: Children's Press, 1992.

Parker, Barbara K. *North American Wolves.* Minneapolis: Carolrhoda, 1998.

Schneider, Jost. *Lynx.* Minneapolis: Carolrhoda, 1995.

Souza, D. M. *It's a Mouse!* Minneapolis: Carolrhoda, 1998.

Winner, Cherie. *Woodpeckers.* Minneapolis: Carolrhoda, 2001.

Websites

Coniferous Forests < http://www.panda.org/kids/wildlife /mnconife.htm

The World Wildlife Federation's site offers a description of the plants and animals of the boreal forest.

Educational in Nature < http://www.gp.com/EducationalinNature /topics/index.html

Georgia-Pacific presents this site with facts about the make-up of a forest, forest ecosystems, and, of course, forest products.

Pukaskwa National Park
< http://parkscanada.pch.gc.ca/parks
/ontario/pukaskwa/pukaskwa_e.htm

This park in Ontario, Canada, is next to Lake Superior. The site features practical information about visiting the park, a virtual tour of the park, and photographs of boreal forest plants, wildlife, and other natural phenomena.

Superior National Forest—Forest Displays
< http://www.snf.toofarnorth.org/displays/ >

This site includes links to information about the boreal forest, health of a forest, fires, black bears, raccoons, and the International Wolf Center in Ely, MN.

Taiga Biome
< http://mbgnet.mobot.org/sets/taiga/index .htm

This site from the Evergreen Project describes plants and animals of the boreal forest. There is an account of a student's trip to the boreal forest of Alaska.

Photo Acknowledgments

The images in this book are used with the permission of: Visuals Unlimited: (© Gary W. Carter) pp. 4–5, (© Wally Eberhart) pp. 9, 14–15, 18 (top), (© Steve Maslowski) pp. 10, 24, (© B. J. Barton) p. 11, (© Peter Ziminski) p. 12, (© Kirtley-Perkins) p. 13, (© Michael S. Quinton) pp. 16 (top), 22, (© Doug Sokell) pp. 19, 38, (© Tom J. Ulrich) pp. 20, 36, 40, (© W. J. Weber) p. 21, (© Joe McDonald) pp. 23, 31, 41, 44, (© Will Troyer) p. 25, (© Leonard Lee Rue III) pp. 27, 29, (© John Sohlden) p. 30, (© Elizabeth DeLaney) p. 33, (© R. Lindholm) p. 35, (© Glen Oliver) p. 39, (© Dick Scott) p. 42, (© Beth Davidow) p. 43, (© Garry Walter) p. 45; © Gary Braasch, pp. 6, 7, 16 (bottom), 18 (bottom); © Kent and Donna Dannen, p. 17; © Mark Wilson/Wildshot, pp. 26, 37; © Gary Schultz, pp. 28, 32, 34 (bottom); © Daniel J. Cox/ naturalexposures.com, p. 34 (top).

Cover photos by © Daniel J. Cox/ naturalexposures.com (wolf/foreground) and © David Matherly/Visuals Unlimited (trees/background).

Index
Numbers in **bold** refer to photos and drawings.